Night Hunt

Rob Waring, *Series Editor*

THOMSON

—★—™

HEINLE

Australia · Canada · Mexico · Singapore · United Kingdom · United States

Words to Know

This story is set in Botswana, Africa. It happens in the Okavango [oʊkəvɑŋgoʊ] Delta.

Okavango Animals. Here are some animals you will find in the story. Label the pictures with words from the box.

bat-eared fox	frog	gerbil	lion	python

3. _____

4. _____

2. _____

5. _____

1. _____

B Hunting for Food.
Read the paragraph. Complete the sentences with the correct form of the underlined words.

The Okavango Delta is a wetlands area near the Okavango River. There are a lot of wild animals there that live independently of people, including the serval cat. Serval cats usually go hunting at night to catch small animals for food. Serval mothers hunt to feed themselves and their cubs. Servals must be very careful because there are many large predators in the delta as well. Animals, such as lions, and snakes, like the python, sometimes eat servals! In the Okavango Delta, the rule is: 'eat, or be eaten.'

1. A _____ is one name for a young serval cat, lion, etc.

2. _____ means to try to catch and kill an animal or bird for food.

3. A _____ is a low, level area of land near a river.

4. _____ plants, animals, or areas exist in natural conditions.

5. _____ are animals that have long, thin bodies and no legs.

6. A _____ is an animal that hunts, kills, and eats other animals.

A Serval Cat Hunting for Food

Botswana's Okavango Delta is beautiful, **remote**,[1] and wild. The animals here live together each day, as they have always done. Year after year, parents have babies and raise their young ones. When those young animals grow up, they must learn how to live in the wild delta of the Okavango.

One young serval cat is ready to begin this education. He's going out on one of his first independent experiences. Serval cats hunt for food alone, and in the dark of night. This cat is going out into the African night alone for the first time. It's time for his first night hunt.

---

[1] **remote:** a long way from any towns or cities

 CD 1, Track 05

Skim for Gist

**Read through the entire book quickly
to answer the questions.**

1. What is the reader basically about?

2. What animals does the serval cat
   try to hunt?

3. What dangerous animals does he meet?

The serval cat is one of Africa's smallest wild cats, and this young serval is a male. He's about twice as big as an average house cat. However, he lives in a world that is a hundred times more dangerous than a house cat's! For him, the night may be full of good food, but there are also a lot of predators out there. Predators, such as lions, could be hunting for a serval cat to eat for dinner.

Nearby, the serval cat's neighbor, a bat-eared fox, carefully smells the evening air. He's checking for danger. Off in the distance, they hear a lion's **roar**.[2] This reminds both animals that the larger predators control the night. Smaller animals, such as the bat-eared fox and the serval cat, have to be very careful!

---

[2]**roar:** the long, loud, deep sound that a lion makes

Bat-Eared Fox

The young serval begins his hunt. Each evening, the serval will have a very important test. He must eat, but he must also escape being eaten at the same time. These are difficult tasks for a young animal **on his own**.[3] The serval cat is still a beginner at hunting. He has to learn this important skill quickly, or he will always have to go hungry.

---

[3]**on (one's) own:** alone; not protected by others

Gerbils are an important part of the menu for serval cats, and this cat suddenly finds a pair of gerbils in the grass. The night hunt begins! Every move the gerbils make is heard by the serval cat's big ears. The cat jumps high above the tall grass as he follows the frightened gerbils' quick movements. A serval can jump as high as **12 feet**[4] in the air to catch a flying bird—or a gerbil in the grass— if he has the skill.

---

[4]**12 feet:** 3.65 meters (1 foot = 0.3048 meters)

A serval cat can jump up to 12 feet in the air!

Unfortunately, this young serval doesn't quite have what he needs to catch anything—at least not yet. The young male isn't as fast as the gerbils and they quickly escape into the tall grass. It looks like the young serval may go hungry. However, the gerbils may not be as lucky as we thought. One serval's loss may be another serval's gain.

Infer Meaning

1. What does the writer mean by 'at least not yet'?

2. What does the saying 'one serval's loss may be another serval's gain' mean?

The unlucky gerbils have run right into the range of an adult female serval cat and her two cubs. These cats are also really hungry. The female welcomes the chance to teach her babies how to hunt. She guides her young cubs to their dinner, but they must catch it themselves. She's hoping that practice will improve their hunting skills. The first cub takes his turn hunting the gerbils. He's easily successful, and happily goes off into the night with his meal.

Next it's the other cub's chance. The young cub carefully **stalks**[5] his **prey**.[6] Finally he jumps—he gets it! With their mother's help, these serval cats have gotten some of the quickest and easiest meals they will ever catch. No one knows that better than the first young serval; he's alone and hungry in the night.

---

[5]**stalk:** follow carefully and closely; usually in order to catch or kill
[6]**prey:** an animal that is hunted and killed for food by another

For the young serval, the night isn't finished yet, and he continues to hunt for his own meal. The delta has got a lot of gerbils—millions of them in fact—and they should be easy to catch. That is, if certain unwelcome guests keep away.

The young serval soon finds another gerbil and dinner seems very close. Then a big problem suddenly arrives. A lion! All of the animals in the area, including the bat-eared fox and the serval, quickly decide to leave. The lion is a very dangerous predator for these small animals.

It's already been a hard night for the young serval. There have been speedy gerbils that get away and noisy lions that **interrupt**[7] the hunt. What else can go wrong? Suddenly there's the sound of **thunder**[8] in the distance—rain!

---

[7]**interrupt:** stop an action; usually not in a polite way
[8]**thunder:** a sudden loud noise from the sky in a rainstorm

Luckily, it's a short storm, and afterwards, there's a bit of activity at a local **pond.**[9] The animals have started to come out again after the rain, so the serval decides to have a look. Right now for the young serval, anything that moves looks good to eat. As he approaches the pond, he finds something unexpected. It's a huge frog! It takes experience and skill to catch a meal this fast and wet. Still, the serval decides that anything is worth trying to hunt at least once. Unfortunately for the serval, the frog stays in the water and it's just too wet for him to catch it this time.

_____

[9]**pond:** an area of water smaller than a lake

The serval finds something he didn't expect at the pond.

The young serval decides to rest after his big adventure, but he soon rises to continue his hunt. He's hungry, and the young cat's first night hunt in the Okavango is not going very well. He decides to try his luck at the pond once again. There are no frogs around the pond when he arrives. However, this time, something different is moving in the water—something much bigger and more dangerous than a frog!

It's a giant python! The serval has never met a snake as big as this one before. He may not know how dangerous it is. The serval decides to take a closer look at this new and interesting discovery. If the serval goes too near the python, the python could kill him.

The young serval slowly gets closer and closer to the huge snake. Suddenly, the python **strikes**![10] The cat reacts quickly and the snake's long teeth miss him. He tries to get closer to the dangerous python one more time. The snake quickly strikes again; it just misses the serval's foot. Finally, the young serval decides that he's learned enough about the dangerous animal and he slowly backs away. It's a good decision!

---

[10]**strike:** reach out suddenly; usually to hurt something or someone

The serval doesn't know just how dangerous the python is!

For the young serval cat, it has been a long, difficult night. But it could have been a lot rougher—and a lot shorter—at least he's still alive. It's better to be hungry than to be food for something else. This is an important rule for every predator in the Okavango Delta: "Eat, or be eaten."

It's time for the young serval to go home. He's hungry, but he's also tired. Other animals are just waking, but he must go to sleep and get some rest. Tomorrow will be another chance for an exciting night hunt!

Sequence the Events

What is the correct order of the events? Write numbers.

_____ The serval hunts a pair of gerbils.

_____ The serval discovers a python.

_____ Two serval cubs catch gerbils.

_____ The serval finds a frog.

_____ A lion frightens the serval.

After You Read

1. In paragraph 1 on page 4, the phrase 'their young ones' refers to:
   A. serval cats
   B. parents
   C. human babies
   D. baby animals

2. According to page 7, what is the biggest danger for a serval?
   A. predators
   B. other serval cats
   C. house cats
   D. the darkness

3. Which of the following is a good heading for page 8?
   A. Fox and Cat Make Friends
   B. Lion Lost in the Night
   C. Smaller Animals Must Be Careful
   D. Small Predators Control the Night

4. According to page 11, the young serval _____ learn how to hunt quickly.
   A. can
   B. won't
   C. does
   D. must

5. What is the main purpose of page 12?
   A. to show how fast the serval cat learns
   B. to explain the skills a serval cat needs to hunt
   C. to show how clever gerbils are
   D. to show the cat's mistakes

6. On page 14, the word 'escape' can be replaced by:
   A. get away
   B. climb over
   C. run up
   D. go down

7. On page 16, how did the serval cubs catch the gerbils successfully?
   A. The gerbils came directly to them.
   B. They had fun running and jumping.
   C. Their mother helped them.
   D. The gerbils were asleep.

8. The serval cat decides to leave the area _____ seeing a lion.
   A. when
   B. at
   C. to
   D. after

9. According to page 19, which of the following makes the serval's hunt difficult?
   A. rain
   B. fast gerbils
   C. a lion
   D. all of the above

10. On page 20, what's the meaning of the word 'unexpected'?
   A. surprising
   B. nice
   C. normal
   D. exciting

11. On page 24, why does the writer say, "It's a good decision!"?
   A. because the serval is too young to try to eat a python
   B. because the serval can come back another time
   C. because if the serval stays he will probably be hurt
   D. because the serval is hurt and must find safety

12. Which of the following is the best part of the night for the serval?
   A. He found lots of food.
   B. He's still alive.
   C. He met some new animals.
   D. He can go home to sleep.

Should We Keep Wild Animals as Pets?

A Discussion with Two Experts

Judy: Hello. This is Judy Jamison again, with our weekly talk show. Today we're discussing wild animals as pets. Our guests are Dr. Russell Baker, a biology teacher at Worth University, and Dr. John Phillips, an animal doctor who works at the Park Animal Hospital. Let's start with you, Dr. Phillips. Some people say that wild animals are too dangerous to keep in the home, but you disagree. Why?

Dr. Phillips: There are a lot of untrue stories about these animals as pets. When people treat wild animals correctly, they are no more dangerous than any other pet. Last week someone brought in a giant snake that was as gentle as a baby cat. He was really sweet. In the last month, I've seen foxes, lions, frogs, and even a bear cub. They were all perfect pets.

Judy: Thank you, Dr. Phillips. Now, Dr. Baker, what do you think?

Animal	Food	Other Needs	Special Problems
Ball Python	only eats live animals, usually mice	needs a warm hiding place to feel safe	can grow to five feet in length
Lion	only eats uncooked meat, and a lot of it!	needs a very large living space	owning a pet lion is only legal in certain countries
African Frog	will eat small fish, and cat or dog food	needs a ready supply of fresh water	may escape often; strong cover needed for living area

Special Needs of Wild Animals

Dr. Baker: I totally disagree. For one thing, many of these animals are hurt when they are taken from the wild. It's a terribly frightening experience for them. Also, in someone's home, they don't have the freedom and space they need to move around. It is not healthy for them. And, on the subject of health, some wild animals also carry serious diseases.

Judy: Interesting point. Dr. Phillips, what can people do to be certain that both their wild pets and their families are healthy and safe?

Dr. Phillips: Well, Dr. Baker is right. There are dangers involved with owning wild animals as a pets. Most of these animals have special needs that must be considered. But if they are addressed properly, the pleasure that these animals bring is worth the time and care that they demand.

Judy: And we'll be discussing those special needs right after we take a short break. We'll be right back!

CD 1, Track 06

Word Count: 367
Time: _____

Vocabulary List

bat-eared fox (2, 8, 9, 19)

cub (3, 16, 27)

delta (2, 3, 4, 19, 27)

frog (2, 20, 23, 27)

gerbil (2, 12, 14, 16, 19, 27)

hunt (3, 4, 7, 11, 12, 16, 19, 23, 27)

interrupt (19)

lion (2, 3, 7, 8, 19, 27)

on (one's) own (11)

pond (20, 21, 23)

predator (3, 7, 8, 19)

prey (16)

python (2, 3, 24, 25, 27)

remote (4)

roar (8)

serval (cat) (3, 4, 7, 8, 11, 12, 13, 14, 15, 16, 19, 20, 21, 23, 24, 25, 27)

stalk (16)

strike (24)

thunder (19)

wild (3, 4, 7)